T0197183

LOSS

A PRACTICAL GUIDE FOR COPING WITH LOSS

MICHAEL P PIERCE

BALBOA.
PRESS

A DIVISION OF HAY HOUSE

Balboa Press books may be ordered through booksellers or by contacting:

Balboa Press
A Division of Hay House
1663 Liberty Drive
Bloomington, IN 47403
www.balboapress.com.au
1 (877) 407-4847

Because of the dynamic nature of the Internet, any web addresses or
links contained in this book may have changed since publication and
may no longer be valid. The views expressed in this work are solely those
of the author and do not necessarily reflect the views of the publisher,
and the publisher hereby disclaims any responsibility for them.

The author of this book does not dispense medical advice or prescribe the use
of any technique as a form of treatment for physical, emotional, or medical
problems without the advice of a physician, either directly or indirectly. The
intent of the author is only to offer information of a general nature to help
you in your quest for emotional and spiritual well-being. In the event you use
any of the information in this book for yourself, which is your constitutional
right, the author and the publisher assume no responsibility for your actions.

Any people depicted in stock imagery provided by Thinkstock are
models, and such images are being used for illustrative purposes only.
Certain stock imagery © Thinkstock.

Print information available on the last page.

ISBN: 978-1-5043-0153-4 (sc)
ISBN: 978-1-5043-0154-1 (e)

Balboa Press rev. date: 02/19/2016

CONTENTS

Foreword vii
Personal Notes about this book ix
Introduction xi

Types of Loss.. 1
Turning loss into growth 4
Grieving over Dying and Death 9
Grieving over Suicide.. 14
Good Grief vs Bad Grief 16
Turning Darkness into Light 20
The Three Step model explained...............................25
Unhealthy Responses to Loss....................................30
Moral Inventory 35
Honesty and Truth 39
Grieving over Relationships 43
Positive Mental Attitudes 58
Taking Positive Actions...60
How to Mend a Wounded Heart 62
Setting and Achieving Realistic Goals.......................66
Do's for Recovery 68
Don'ts for Recovery...72
Positive Thoughts for Today and Always...................74
Winners Are People like You 76
A Reflection on our Life's Journey.............................78
An Affirmation for your Journey 80

CONTENTS

Foreword

This book is dedicated to you and/or to someone you know who could use some practical help in overcoming loss.

It is also dedicated to all the counselors, therapists, ministers, doctors, psychologists, families and friends who recommend or purchase this book in the knowledge that it can help those who may need some practical help and simple advice in overcoming their loss and grief at this point or perhaps at another point in their lives.

It is especially dedicated to my brother, Laurence Pierce who has been an inspiration to me for many years, as well as many others who have come into contact with him in the course of his unselfish work in helping others in their journey through life.

It is also dedicated to the many people who have helped me along the way, by their emotional support, encouragement and their sharing of the grief that they have experienced in their lives. I would need to write another book just to mention their names, so I am sure they will understand if I do not specifically mention their names here, but hopefully, they all know that they have helped others and me by their caring and sharing.

And lastly it is dedicated to my wife Paula whom I have learned more about pure love, commitment, honesty, compassion, communication, and relationships from more than I have from anyone else. Paula lives out her values and principles on a daily basis, with everyone whom she comes into contact with. She is a shining example to me and to all as to what integrity is all about. Thank you Paula for motivating me to complete this book.

Personal Notes about this book

This is a non-academic self-help book intended for general readership. It is not intended to be an academic reference book and as such, I have not referenced the countless research documents and books that have influenced me in writing this book.

It is now very easy for anyone to research the subjects in this book in their own time and with the help of the Internet.

I have made references to sources where I felt it was appropriate and to give due credit to the originators of material and concepts that were created by others.

All of the quotes in this book (that are not referenced to others) are my quotes.

You can interpret references to God and Prayer in any way that you wish and whatever feels comfortable for you. You may not believe in a Divine Creator or in the power of prayer. You may prefer to call prayer 'positive affirmations'. You may be an agnostic, an atheist, a spiritual person or not. It doesn't matter what your spiritual beliefs or non-beliefs are. It is my hope that you and many others will find that this book will be helpful regardless of your beliefs.

Important: The information and self-help resources in this book are not intended to be a substitute for mental health assessment, medical or psychiatric consultation, assessment or treatment.

Introduction

Do you feel or do you know anyone who has the following feelings?

- Sadness
- Gloom
- Depression
- Sorrow
- Anxiety
- Fear
- Lack of confidence
- Tiredness
- Grief
- Loneliness
- Isolation
- Unhappiness
- Anger
- Guilt
- A wounded heart
- Rejection
- Despair
- Panic
- Emotionally flat
- Illness

- Disbelief
- Nervous
- Confused
- Low in spirit
- Abandoned
- Betrayed
- Tearful
- Worried
- Panic attacks
- Unsure about the future

The list could go on, but the above list is long enough to be aware of some of the normal feelings people feel when they are going through a sense of loss of any kind.

The objective of this book is to help any reader overcome these feeling of doom and gloom and to help them move forward to peace, joy, contentment and wellness, (if they simply decide to apply what they read in this book).

This book is intended to be helpful in a very basic, easy and practical way. To some who read this book, they may find the contents obvious, but it is always the most obvious that we overlook, forget and fail to apply. Some readers may accept in their own minds that the principles, ideas and suggestions in this book make good sense, but a word of caution, if they are not applied, they won't help anyone! I invite you as a reader of this book to start applying the fundamentals in it now! It will not only help you to get over loss, it will bless your life abundantly, enrich it and bring you much pleasure, peace and joy!

Types of Loss

Loss comes in many forms. We are all familiar with the concept of loss and grief following a death, and while some readers might be facing this type of loss right now, others may be feeling countless other forms of loss. It may surprise many readers to discover what can constitute a tragic loss to a person and as a result that person may be going through the same grieving process and stages encountered by a person who loses someone close to them through death.

Unfortunately, some of us experience multiple losses at the same time. This is more challenging to deal with. In addition to a death loss, there are many others.

In fact, loss can be the loss of anything dear to us that gave us pleasure, security, familiarity, meaning, purpose, happiness and joy.

Redundancy and the fear and insecurity that it causes can be overwhelming. Loss of health and having to give up things that gave us much pleasure can be very difficult to come to terms with.

Separation of any kind is as close as you can get to a death loss experience and often it can be worse for many people because the one/s they lost are still alive and that can make it more difficult to get over.

Breakups in families through a divorce can be as painful if not more painful because divorce breakups can involve more than one loss. Other losses can include the loss of your partner/

companion/friends, and the loss of your children, extended families and associated friends.

Even the loss or death of a pet can set us back, particularly for those whose only close friend and companion was their loyal and faithful pet.

There's the loss of a friend or family member to alcohol or drug abuse. There's the loss of a family member to a life of crime and/or incarceration, and God forbid, the unbearable grieving loss of a family member or friend through suicide.

Some people have to move away from their familiar surroundings, family and friends, in order to find work far away from their home. These people all go through a grieving process. Families, who have to sell up and move for economic reasons, also go through feelings of loss that extends to the whole family. Children have to leave school, and start all over again to make new friends in new and strange surroundings to them. The whole family's entire and familiar support network is lost because of the forced move.

Some unfortunate people have to move because of some disaster such as drought, flood, or fire. People in this unfortunate situation have more than one form of grief to deal with and we less burdened should count our blessings that we have been spared the depth of losses others have had or are experiencing at the moment.

Just think of some of the tragedies that some people have had to suffer through, such as when a large part of a family has been lost in a tragic accident or a disaster of some kind.

Reflect for just a moment on what some entire families are going through in war torn countries where they have lost absolutely everything. And then for some of them who manage to escape those war torn countries as refugees, they end up losing their family at sea, while attempting to flee from oppression, persecution or poverty, when all they wanted was a chance of a new start and a new beginning in another country.

There is a great deal of loss, suffering, and sadness around us and all over the world. This can help us to put into perspective whatever we are going through at the moment. This self-help book looks at the practical steps we can take to change those things that we can have control over and to help us and others move forward to a brighter and happier future.

We are all in some way touched by loss, and as a result, we all can do with as much help as possible, whether it is at this precise moment in time or at some other time in the future. We can all do with plenty of advice, help, support and encouragement when it comes to the dealing with loss of any kind.

Other forms of loss include, but are not limited to:

- Relationship breakups, separation and divorce
- Job, career, redundancy
- Health, disability
- Youthfulness, coming to terms with dying
- Home
- Money
- Investments
- Loss of a Business
- Security
- Friend/s
- Family
- Community, status, roles and involvement
- Social networks
- Fitness and agility, loss of energy
- Hobbies, pastimes, sport and other activities
- Eyesight, hearing, use of a limb/s, memory
- Loss of a pet
- Children leaving home
- Having to move, or immigrate
- Loss of personal possessions
- Physical beauty
- Confidence
- Peace of mind
- Losses associated with Retirement
- Losses from Growing old
- Losses as a result of an Injury

Turning loss into growth

"LOSS CAN BE A LIFE TRANSFORMING PROCESS"

The above quotation can be hard for a reader who has never experienced real loss before. To get their head around the idea that loss can be a life transforming process and despite the grief that they may be experiencing at the moment, the quotation is never the less true. In time, the reader will look back and realize this.

With loss comes grief. Grief is a process that takes each person grieving through stages. Most people go through similar stages, some more, some less. The common stages are:

> **Shock, Disbelief, Sadness, Upset, Anger, Guilt, Fear, Lack of confidence, Resentment, Bitterness, Acceptance, Letting go and Moving on,** to new experiences and new joys in their lives.

Loss and grief and their associated feelings and moods will come to everyone sooner or later. And for most of us, we will experience these feelings/moods many times in our lifetime.

Both loss and growth are two of the most natural and fundamental experiences and processes that every human being will go through at various times in their lives. They are not aspects of our lives that we constantly think about every day. They are always in the background, they are always ready to surface to our consciousness, and it's just a matter of time before they do.

We all start out in life with our first experience of loss when we are born. We leave the comfort, warmth and security of our mother's womb, we feel disrupted, and uncomfortable. This is why babies cry at birth.

In our crib, when we are put down to sleep, we cry from a sense of separation. When the lights are turned off, we cry in fear and because of separation and the loss of personal contact with our mother or father. Even as we grow older in infancy, we still feel this way for a long time until we work out that our protectors are close at hand. So you see, we start to experience loss from the day we are born, and guess what? It is a natural feeling! Loss is never a happy experience, but it can be a growing experience.

Most people around us, during and after our birth, don't feel any loss at all. They feel growth, joy, happiness, (and perhaps parental tiredness). But for you, at certain times, despite everyone else's joy and happiness, when you want attention rather than sleep and when the light is turned off, you feel scared, insecure and a temporary sense of loss. As a child, your feelings of loss are not rational, but to you, they are real.

Life and death, loss and growth are natural and normal patterns of life and our universe. They are two sides of the same coin. Nature supplies us with abundant examples. For instance, leaves fall off a tree in autumn and die, to be replaced by fresh new green leaves in the springtime. The caterpillar goes into its own cocoon in order to die and emerge in a new life as a beautiful butterfly.

Our own bodies start dying from the day we are born. Our external skin cells die and fall off our body to be replaced by new skin. Our hair falls out to be replaced by new hair follicles. Our cells are constantly regenerating themselves all the time, death and life, loss and growth.

As we move from infancy, we reach a time for going to school. We experience many of the emotions and fears associated with loss. Yet, these initial experiences of fear and loss eventually turn into experiences of growth, confidence, and joy. We make friends, have fun, and sometimes, are enjoying ourselves so much in the playground after school that we don't want to go home. This is an example of moving from fear to joy, from a feeling of loss to gain.

In young adulthood, we find girlfriends/boyfriends, we form close alliances, develop our friendships, and then sometimes things happen and some of these relationships break down. This is an example of loss.

As we grow older we get a job and sometimes the job doesn't work out so we may feel an experience of loss.

Then there comes a time when we fall in love and experience intimacy for the first time. Things are going great. You are happy, content and feeling on top of the world. But, something happens, and it all falls apart. When this happens you will experience many of the feelings associated with loss and grief.

These experiences will be more traumatic when you have married the person you fell in love with and even more so when you have had children together.

So, perhaps you have managed to get over your failed marriage. Perhaps you have moved on and found the ideal job, which has helped to take your mind off of your grief. You think that you are now gaining some stability in your life and the job that has been helping to keep you going is taken away from you through economic conditions, insolvency or redundancy. This is another great loss experience.

Then as you are getting over your previous losses in life, your father or mother dies unexpectedly. A parent that you fell out with and had not seen for a long time. Well of course you had your own life to live. You had your own problems to deal with, and kept meaning to make contact with him or her, and now you will be making contact with him or her at their funeral.

This unexpected situation may cause you tremendous grief, guilt and sadness, which are just some of the feelings that you may go through.

The above scenarios are just a few examples of what many of us may go through in our life journey. They are by no means complete and some of the examples may not apply to you at all. I am sure you will relate to your own experiences of loss and grief.

In fact, change of any kind brings a sense of loss, even when we are expecting the change and are feeling optimistic about it.

Take for example parents looking forward to when their kids leave home to go to college, or just leave home for any reason. Once the time comes and when they walk out the door, you may feel overcome by a sense of loss.

When you leave a job of your own accord and have another exciting job lined up, when you walk out of the office, you may feel a sense of grief.

Our losses are unique to each of us because of what they represented to us. We are losing connections we have made that may have shaped our lives. We may be losing people we admired, mentors, loyal friends, advisors, people and patterns that have played an important part in making us who we have become.

We connect losses with our values, principles and morals. We may associate our losses with losing a part of our identity, and with who we are. We may have invested a great deal of time, effort and energy into what was symbolic to us such as a job or a relationship and this can have a significant impact on us. The loss may not only shake us but may cause depression and anxiety that may need professional help and counseling.

Unfortunately we do not realize how much meaning we have invested in something or someone until we lose them. It's all a matter of how we deal with and cope with the loss that matters most. It's what we learn from the loss and how we apply what we have learned from the loss that is of the utmost importance.

"With every loss there are always new beginnings"

As our experiences of loss are unique to each of us, so will our responses be. But, there is a difference between our responses and how we cope. Our responses will be similar in many respects, but we may use different coping mechanisms. You may have some that are not included in this book, and that is great, if they don't include alcohol, drugs or deviant distractions. On the other-hand, if you just begin to apply even some of the suggestions in this book, they will help you in ways beyond your grief. Try them and discover for yourself.

There are as many unhealthy ways of coping as there are healthy ways. Hold on to the healthy ways and discard the unhealthy ways.

Don't shut yourself off from the world and retreat to your room and drink yourself to death in your sorrow. Discard sayings that may have been drummed into you mind that "Big boys don't cry" "Girls can be as strong as men", "Don't be such a sissy", "Keep your feelings to yourself", "Expressing your feelings is a sign of weakness", and so on.

Facing your ghosts and your negative influences is part of the process. In fact, you must give them up as your first step to recovery. You need to decide to let go of and loose those habits and patterns that have not been serving you well and replace them with positive and healthy habits that will lead to your recovery and a new life!

Grieving over Dying and Death

When someone is facing death as a result of a terminal illness, they usually sense it. Some will accept their fate and plan accordingly; others will fight it to the end. There is no right or wrong way to approach death, apart from ensuring that when it comes, it will be dignified. Each of us will have to go through our own journey in facing up to a terminal illness or a death, and no one can tell us what we should or should not feel. The most important thing for all concerned is to be honest about the prognosis and the likely outcome. This does not mean that hope should be abandoned, because miracles do and can happen. It is a matter of being as prepared as we can to face up to the likely outcome of the terminal illness, should that be the challenge.

The best thing for a terminally ill person to do is to talk about their predicament and the best thing for those who are close to a terminally ill person is to engage them in conversation about their situation, rather than covering it up and avoiding it.

In Elisabeth Kubler-Ross's book *On Death and Dying*, she urges us to open up a dialogue with those who are terminally ill. As a psychiatrist, she describes the enormous relief provided to the dying when they are invited to share their fears and their needs at this most sensitive and dramatic stage of their life. She maintains that engaging the dying in constant dialogue will greatly ease their journey toward death and help them to face it with acceptance rather than fear. This should be the primary objective for both the dying and those close to them.

A pending death journey is divided into five basic stages. Some will experience more and some will experience less, but to keep things uncomplicated, it is generally accepted by professionals that these are the most common stages. And for some people, they may not go through these stages in the order presented here. For some, it will be a frightening roller coaster experience of emotions in no rational or particular order.

The five basic stages are:

Denial that this is happening is usually the first response when one receives the news of a terminal illness. "I don't believe it!" "The results might be wrong?" "Let's have more tests done".

Anger at people, sometimes the doctor and carers. Anger and upset at life in general for allowing this to happen. Anger over missed opportunities and "Why Me?"

Bargaining in our minds with God in an attempt to postpone the inevitable. Promises to God that I promise to become a better person if I get better, or "Please Dear Lord, just give me another ten years and I will then be happy to go gracefully".

Depression about our fate, opportunities missed, unfinished business, feelings about what we are losing and preparing to mourn over our own pending death, which we consider to be the greatest loss feeling anyone could ever have.

Acceptance is the last stage of the pending death journey and experience for most terminally ill people. Sometimes they communicate that they are now ready to die, sometimes they accept it internally without mentioning it and eventually just drift off to the afterlife in their sleep or whilst in a coma. Dr Kubler-Ross concludes that when a dying person is assisted with the first four stages of dying that they will release their anger, fear and depression and will contemplate their ending with a certain degree of quiet expectation. Our greatest gift to the dying is to be with them in silence and in words, and they will teach us what to do.

Some tips for helping the dying.

There are all kinds of things that we can do to help anyone who is facing death. The main thing is to be there for them as often as we can and as often as they would like us to be with them. Sometimes when a terminally ill person is in a lot of pain, not looking their best and may be hooked up to machines, they may be reluctant to see people. This is understandable and should be respected, at least for a short period of time, because modern medicine these days can normally prevent physical pain by the administration of painkillers.

When it comes to dealing with a woman who is terminally ill, if the patient wishes, a nice thing to do might be to arrange visits by a hair stylist and to arrange for the application of make up to help the female patient look their best. Fresh flowers in the room would be nice.

If the patient is up to it, it might be nice to get as many people as possible to visit the patient, especially long lost friends and family members. Bring books on spirituality and subjects relating to death and dying that may help the patient, especially if they express an inclination to read such material. When the company of friends and family leave, the patient often feels a great sense of loneliness and these types of books can help occupy their minds and prepare them for what they are going through and what they are facing.

If the patient is religious, they may appreciate visits from a minister of their religion or a grief counsellor who is trained in these matters.

There will always be help required to get their affairs in order and this can be a tremendous help and relieve them from unnecessary stress as they have enough to deal with on their plate.

The greatest sadness for the dying is the grief of things left undone and sorrow for mistakes made and the hurt they may have caused others in the past. If there is anything that you can do to help them make things right before they die, this would be a supreme help to them. It may be that you can invite a family member or a close friend whom they fell out with because of some past incident.

There may have been some things that they always wanted to do but never did. If there is any practical way that you are able to arrange for it to be done now and they are able to experience it, you should do everything in your power to try and organise it. I remember being in a respite home and was amazed to see a terminally ill man, who also happened to be a paraplegic, sipping beer through a straw. On enquiry, I found out from the nurse that he had never taken a drink in his life and when asked if he had any final wishes, he replied that he would love to try a beer. Under the circumstances his wish was granted, and the doctor authorised the nurses to give him all the beer he wanted. This is in fact what happened. A little fridge was installed beside his bed that was full of cold cans of beer and whenever he felt like one, he would ring his buzzer and a smiling nurse would promptly appear, open a beer for him, put a straw in the can and let him sip away to his heart's content. I am not advocating that people take up drinking when they know they are going to die, but in this case it was entirely appropriate. After all, he only had a few weeks to live and the beer diminished his sadness and he died with a smile on his face.

The next example will be uncomfortable to some, but I share it to make the point that if there is anything that we can do to relieve the anxiety and depression of the dying we should do it even if it contravenes taboos and other peoples dislikes.

I know of a man who was dying from lung cancer. He was in hospital and acknowledged the fact that he was dying. And even though he was dying as a result of being a lifetime heavy smoker, right up to the end, he couldn't overcome the addiction he had, and when people came to visit him, he would ask them to wheel him outside the hospital where he could have a smoke. This helped him cope with his pending death, it helped to relax him and knowing that he was beyond hope of a miracle in his case; people bit their tongues and granted him his last wishes.

It may be that sometimes when you visit the dying that they may not feel like talking. If that is the case, simply sit with them and hold their hand in silence. Just being there can make all the difference. Sometimes, you may just sit and cry with them.

"Sometimes crying is as good as laughter".

There may be times when a dying person simply cannot bear to face people for many reasons, and if this happens, the person's wishes must be respected. However, occasionally, the dying patient may put up a barrier to communicating and claim that they don't want to see anyone. Often, this is just to see who cares enough to break the barriers down and secretly it is often a silent cry from them to find someone who can push through their barriers and help to pull them out of their deep depression.

The person, who can do this, is truly an Angel!

For people dying who have had a strong faith, it can be very comforting for them to focus on their belief in an afterlife of eternal peace and joy. A belief that they are not only going to meet their maker, but that they will meet up with loved ones who have already departed this life. This can even include their faithful pet that has passed on. A belief that all of those who have gone before them will be there waiting for them at the gates of heaven with smiling faces and open arms waiting to greet them. Even those who hurt them in the past, and their past enemies who have died, will now be among those waiting for them in a place of bliss where only pure love, peace and joy exists for all.

The greatest stressor in life is the death of a close family member or a partner. Parallel to this stressor is facing pending death ourselves, through a terminal illness or injury. We will all face death in one way or another at some stage in our lives. In America alone, eight million people, every year, experience death in a family. Every year, there are approx. 1000000 new widows and widowers. Every year, approximately half a million children and young people die before they reach the age of twenty-five.

It is prudent therefore to be aware of what will come to visit us sooner or later and to be sensitive to the stress it can cause us and those around us. It may be that the other types of losses referred to in this book, can be as traumatic as a death loss experience.

Grieving over Suicide

In Australia alone, someone attempts to take his or her life every 10 minutes. On a worldwide basis, the figures are staggering. Suicide is like cancer in the sense that everyone knows someone who is affected by these dreaded diseases.

However, suicide is preventable, if the tendency is recognised and if help is sought by the person contemplating suicide, and those who know or suspect that the tendency exists.

Suicide is the intent to cause one's own death as a result of a feeling of hopelessness and/or worthlessness. It's a mental disorder that can be brought on by despair, severe depression, alcohol, drugs, bi-polar disorder, schizophrenia, and other mental illnesses, relationship problems, and any situation that causes an overwhelming sense of doom and gloom.

It is an illness that causes an inability to rationalise, an inability to think clearly and it makes it difficult for the sufferer to feel a sense of hope and optimism for the future.

It is estimated that 1 million people die, worldwide, as a result of suicide each year, making it the tenth leading cause of death worldwide. Males make up 80% of this figure. There are an estimated 20 million attempted suicides each year worldwide.

50% of people who attempt suicide have a genetic predisposition, which means that these people need extra help to cope with their predisposition.

HELP is the key word, for those contemplating suicide and for those close to them who may be aware of their situation. It is both a personal obligation to help oneself and a societal obligation to help those vulnerable to a disease that is preventable.

Loss of some kind is the catalyst that drives people to suicide. It is my hope that the contents of this book will play an important part in preventing suicide and helping those who have lost someone to suicide get over their grief, pain and suffering.

I cannot overstate the need for seeking professional help in this area. The brain chemistry of someone who is contemplating suicide may need to be put back into balance and this will often require prescribed medications by a professional medical doctor as well as counselling and a great deal of support from friends and family.

Please phone help-lines and seek counselling and medical advice for anyone you suspect is prone or vulnerable to suicide, especially if it happens to be yourself!

Never ever judge anyone who has suicidal tendencies or who has died as a result of them. These people need our help and understanding in that they are finding it hard to cope, and may have sadly decided death over life because of their inability to deal with loss of some kind. It is our duty to help in every way we can.

In Australia, phone: Lifeline and Beyond Blue for free telephone counselling.

In all other countries: Phone Suicide telephone help lines which can be found on the Internet. These help lines give free advice and can help save lives.

Good Grief vs Bad Grief

Grieving is normal, healthy and part of the natural process we will all go through after we experience a loss of some kind. Despite our feelings of sadness, anxiety and depression, I call this normal grieving process 'Good Grief'.

Loss and growth, grief and joy precede each other in the cycles of life and nature. An example of this in nature is the minor feelings of sadness when summer comes to an end, the bright summer days and long balmy evenings and beautiful sunsets make way for longer colder and darker days of winter. We may be fortunate to have a summer cottage or beach house that we start to close down in the autumn in preparation for the onset of winter. We may feel a slight sense of sadness as we pack our belongings and say goodbye to the happy memories of the summer season among family and friends in the warmth of the summer sun. Adults prepare to return to work and perhaps mundane jobs and the kids prepare to return to school and their studies and the daily routines of life.

Winter has its joys and pleasures too, but, for most, it's not really the same as the brightness and warmth of the summer season. Yet winter passes along to be replaced by the joy of springtime. Flowers start to bloom. Leaves return to green, and our energy returns along with the happy expectation of the longer brighter days of summer approaching.

When we grieve, we grieve the loss of what something meant to us, not necessarily the lost object itself, or the person, or the season. It's the attachment we associate to the person place or thing that we lose that causes the grief.

With the loss of a person through death, illness, separation or divorce, it's the positive characteristic traits that we miss in the other person that causes our feelings of sadness and grief. Those aspects of their character that we miss such as compassion, companionship, their care and concern for us, their humor, their moral support, their generosity, their presence and their energy, these traits are what we miss because these are traits that we treasure and value in ourselves. In other words, the other person mirrored what is dear to us and in a sense we also feel that we have lost a little bit of ourselves when we lose someone who was very dear to us.

When we lose someone who was very close to us, such as our partner, in a good relationship, or what we perceived as a good relationship, we saw ourselves as a team, a duo, a complete unit made up of each other. When that physical connection is broken, it is normal for us to feel incomplete and a deep sense of loss. We not only feel the loss of connection, but what it represented to us individually and what it may have represented to the outside world. For genuinely great relationships, we lose what that relationship meant to us and the meaning we both invested in it.

Unfortunately, we may not realize how much meaning, energy and time we invested in someone (or the lack of) until we lose them. This is why feelings of 'good grief' are normal, healthy and a necessary part of the process of moving forward. So, moving through the stages of good/healthy grief are necessary, and for some it can be short, and for others it may take longer. It is my hope that once you start applying what you read in this book, as well as other forms of help, the process will be shorter.

Bad grief is unhealthy grief. When you don't go through the healthy stages of grief/separation or when you get stuck in one or more of the stages to the extent that it immobilizes you and you feel trapped and unable to move on, this is unhealthy and may lead to chronic grief. For general loss and grief, excluding death loss, I will take this opportunity to remind you of the stages of healthy 'good grief' and or separation. **N.B. These are slightly different to the 5 death stages referred to earlier. This is a 13 step (non death) model for general grief:**

- Shock
- Disbelief
- Sadness
- Upset
- Anger
- Guilt
- Fear
- Lack of confidence
- Resentment
- Bitterness
- Acceptance
- Letting go
- Moving on

Another shorter model for (non death) stages of loss and grief. This is a 5 step model:

- Denial
- Depression
- Bargaining
- Anger
- Acceptance

My simple 3-step model for coping with loss and grief, a summary of the two models above. These three basic steps are expanded on further in a following chapter.

1. **Acknowledge the loss.**
2. **Accept the reality of the loss**
3. **Take action about the loss.**

Grieving over loss will involve our thoughts, emotions, feelings and our behaviors. Our success in coping with and overcoming loss will depend on how we address these aspects in a healthy manner. Ask yourself if you want to move beyond crippling grief? Your answer and desire will determine your action plan for moving forward.

In a nutshell, my simple three-step model is a condensation of the models above, and others that are floating around and being used by counselors and therapists. It is simple, easy to remember and will help you to focus on the essential steps necessary for a full recovery and a happier, contented and blissful life ahead.

"We have to plan and prepare for the future as that is where we will spend the rest of our lives".

Turning Darkness into Light

"DARKNESS ALWAYS PRECEDES THE LIGHT"

The darkness of night turns into the light of day. The earth spins each and every day from darkness to light. The darkness of winter turns into the brightness of summer. Nature and life are always revolving around the themes of death/loss, life, birth and growth. All the great faiths in the universe address the same themes. Life resurrecting out of death forms the heart of Christianity as it does with other faiths. The body may be buried, or the body may be cremated, but the spirit lives on forever. The death and resurrection of Jesus is a prime example of his spirit living on.

In a quote from the Bible, John 12:24, "Unless a wheat grain falls into the earth and dies, it remains only a single grain; but if it dies it yields a rich harvest". This quotation can be applied to letting go of grief, letting go of habits or patterns of life that don't serve us well, or letting go of relationships that may not have been healthy for us.

An example from nature that relates to this quote is when a single seed is planted in darkness under the ground; it must burst apart from what it was, and push itself up from the darkness towards the sun to become a new form of identity. This is similar to what we need to do in our personal lives. In order to grow, move forward and live again, we need to move from the darkness of our grief to the light of a new life.

I know this seems easier said than done when we are in the middle of grief, but, we have to take control of unhealthy grief instead of letting it take control of us. I also know that there are losses that we have absolutely no control over, however, we do have choices over what we do about them and how we react and respond to them.

We may feel weak, flat, gloomy and depressed, but we still have choices in how we decide to handle unhealthy grief and move forward to wellness in mind, body and spirit.

"It is in the darkest skies that the stars are best seen"
R.P. Evans

We cannot physically turn darkness into light. The heading for this chapter nonetheless is a powerful metaphor. As stated above, we do have choices in how we react to darkness and light, loss and growth. In each of our own experiences of loss, we can choose to move forward towards a fuller life or remain stagnant, and maybe fall backwards towards our own loss of physical and/or emotional health leading in some severe cases to our own death.

Much illness is caused or prolonged due to unresolved loss situations. The majority of patients who visit doctors, counselors, therapists, psychologists and psychiatrists do so because of two conditions, anxiety and depression. The greatest cause of anxiety and depression is loss of some kind.

I have referred earlier to examples of the different types of loss we may go through and this list is by no means a complete list.

It is my opinion that when we choose to get well, we invariably do. When we choose to stay well, we usually do. If we don't want to get well, we will get sick. The choice is yours. You can get the best medical advice and attention available, even the best prescriptions to assist us at times, but until we make up our minds that we want to get well, we probably won't. I beseech you to choose light, life and wellness.

You can and will be forgiven for falling into unhealthy bad grief. After all, nobody teaches us how to handle loss. Most of us go through life focusing only on the positive aspects of our life, falsely believing that in many situations it is just unfortunate or unlucky to have to experience grief and even believing that in some situations it is avoidable and unnecessary.

Those who have not experienced real loss yet, can't understand why we are grieving and turn their backs on us believing that we are weak and wondering why we simply just don't get on with life. These people can hurt us deeply because of their ignorance, insensitivity, lack of understanding and lack of compassion.

We don't learn how to deal with loss from our parents, from our friends, or in school. Insufficient attention has been paid to the role loss plays in life. No one teaches us that the only way new growth comes is through loss. No one teaches us that loss is a normal and natural process in life and that it can't be avoided. No one shows us how to cope with loss. This is the reason why I have written this self-help book.

I recently read about a grieving man who lost his wife after she died while giving birth to their newborn baby. He cried out to the minister who came to visit him afterwards, "Why haven't we been taught how to deal with things like this?"

The answer to this question may be due to the fact that we can't be taught about loss because there is no magic wand that we can wave that will fix everything and make us feel immediately better, but we can, in the course of time, come to terms with the loss by taking the three steps I have referred to earlier, **Acknowledgement, Acceptance, and Action.**

The reason people can't help us completely is probably because they know that it is necessary for us to take these steps ourselves in helping us to overcome our loss. We will need help and support, (as much as we can get) but it is a journey that we will have to experience and get through ourselves, along with the help of others. As tragic, untimely, dreaded and feared death and loss may be, no one will ever be able to avoid them. But, we can begin to accept the losses in our life and learn to grow through them in a constructive and healthy manner. The sooner we begin this process the more prepared we will be and the more able we will be to cope with our present loss and other losses that may come along in the future.

As stated earlier, life is a natural process of loss and re-birth, which means that life, is a process of constantly giving re-birth to ourselves. Choosing to grow and be reborn again through loss now, will enable us to make the same choices again in the future when it will be easier to handle other losses that may come into our lives.

Life is a continuing process of good and bad, ups and downs. Our attitudes play an important part in how we view every situation that we face. We can all handle happiness with open arms, and the good news is that we can also handle the mourning and grief caused by our disappointments, loss and weariness when we realize that these apparent bad times can be transformed into growth.

We mourn over lost opportunities, wrong decisions, lost relationships, lost time and lost precious moments. This is only natural, yet these periods can really be stepping-stones to a fuller life, if we mourn in a healthy way.

It's good to mourn our losses, and part of the healthy process of mourning is to reflect on things that we could have done differently. Perhaps we could have behaved differently, spoken in softer tones, made better use of our time in the past, and so on, but we cannot go back and change anything from the past. We can stay where we are, or we can decide to learn from our reflections and failings. We can choose to make changes to enable us to move forward and not to make the same mistakes again in the future.

Good grief is akin to good sadness. Bad grief on the other hand, is akin to unhealthy bad sadness that can paralyze and immobilize us from living a happy and satisfying life. We need to learn to take control of bad grief, instead of letting it control us.

Unfortunately, bad grief can take over us at times. We get stuck in a time warp. We become morbidly frozen, disheartened and disillusioned by past events that they prevent us from seeing the light at the end of the tunnel. But there is always light at the end of a tunnel, we just have to start walking towards it.

"Behind every cloud is a silver lining"

"There is always light behind every darkness"

"The morning light always follows the darkness of night"

The Three Step model explained

These three steps are also referred to in the chapter, Setting and Achieving Realistic Goals. In reality, the steps nearly always intertwine between each other. In any case, as we move through these basic steps, we will be well on our way to recovery and a renewed life.

"The purpose of life is to accept our imperfections and to grow into our perfection"

Step 1-Acknowledge the loss/s.

Whatever the loss is or was, we must acknowledge it, which simply means facing up to it and taking ownership of it. Recognizing and admitting to ourselves that it has happened. For some this is obvious, but for others, they may get trapped in this first stage by denying or disbelieving the loss. Denial especially in the early stages of loss is normal and healthy. Some people deny for too long and may bargain in their own minds with God that if their loss is returned to them they will become better persons. Take for example the following situations:

- Your partner has left and you sit and wait hoping for their return.

- You lose your job and sit and wait for that phone call (that will never come) from your past employer telling you that you can come back to your job.

- The grieving mother who can't believe her little child has died and keeps cleaning their room in expectation that it was all just a nightmare and her child will return.

The first step in healthy grieving and recovery is when we willingly and openly acknowledge what has been lost. An important healthy component of this step is to start talking to others about how we feel about our loss. Their feedback will be very helpful, encouraging and supportive.

Our first conscious experience of loss may in fact raise previous losses that we buried in our subconscious minds and never really adequately dealt with in the past. I call this **posttraumatic loss distress**. This can temporarily set you back because you may be dealing with a double whammy or even more, as a result of previous unresolved losses.

There may be loss situations from your past, some minor and maybe some more serious, such as sexual abuse, rape, incest, physical and verbal abuse, when at the time you felt a loss of naivety, innocence, dignity, self-respect, or hope, but at that time you either buried your feelings or felt you were strong enough to handle them, and lo and behold, they all come running into your mind now, when for the first time, you find yourself consciously dealing with what you thought was your first real sense of loss.

This is why you need to read this book in its entirety, and if necessary, seek additional help as appropriate to your wellness in mind, body and spirit.

Taking inventory of our history of losses, perhaps for the first time, and despite the brief mental anguish in doing so, will start us on a powerful journey towards discovery, self-awareness, and understanding, which are the fundamental components of the first step of acknowledging our present and previous losses.

Step 2-Accepting the loss/s.

Acknowledging the loss or losses makes it a lot easier to accept the reality of them. Acknowledgement and acceptance are very closely related and usually intertwined. But you can't jump straight into acceptance of a particular loss without going through the acknowledgement step first. For instance, thinking 'Yeah, OK, I accept I was made redundant', or 'Yeah, OK, I accept she/he has left me', 'Yeah, OK, I accept my pet has died', and expect to rush into the last stage without having acknowledged the loss properly and grieved appropriately over it.

By not grieving for an appropriate amount of time, in the first and second steps, by not taking an inventory of your feelings and emotions during these important steps, may keep the present and previous losses under the surface, waiting to emerge at some time in the future, despite your desire to avoid the sadness and possible remorse these emotions and feelings may cause you in facing up to them now, in your quest to get to the final stage as soon as possible.

Our grief during the first two steps needs expression. It needs to be released. Many of us have learned to fear dealing with our emotions because we may feel embarrassed, or that we are weak if we talk about our emotions, feel that we are bothering or troubling others when we openly express how we feel, and so on, so we think we have to be strong, which we equate to being silent and we decide to hide how we really feel. When unexpressed feelings of grief are pushed down into our subconscious minds, they often seek expression in unhealthy ways. Unresolved grief can sour into chronic addictions, self-harm, anger, cynicism, and even violence.

Expressing our emotions is necessary to healthy grieving. The healthy and meaningful expression of our emotions helps us through the grief process and leads to the final stage, at the appropriate time, of taking positive actions in letting go of the past, and its associated pain and sadness, and moving forward to a brighter, fuller and happier future.

"Make your own recovery, the first priority in your life"
Robin Norwood

"Look after your assets, your most
important asset, is yourself"
Mike Pierce

> *"We cannot move forward unless we free*
> *ourselves from the shackles of our past"*
> **Dave Pelzer**

Step 3-Take action about the loss/s

You need to go through steps 1 and 2 before proceeding to this step.

Taking action means positive, healthy constructive actions that speed up your recovery and that will lead to wellness, wholeness and joy in your life again.

> *"Vision without Action is merely a dream*
> *Action without Vision just passes the time*
> *Vision with Action can change our world"*
> **J A Barker**

All conscious actions require goals, in other words, what your vision is, what the objectives are that you would like to achieve. Whatever goal you set for yourself, the beginning, the first step starts with you. Your first step, starts in your own mind. Once you make your mind up and are clear on your objectives, make realistic goals that are within your scope to achieve. There is no sense in fooling yourself that you will be the fastest sprinter in the world, if you don't have the physical attributes that would be required for obtaining such as objective.

Once you have decided on realistic goals that are achievable, list them down and develop a plan on how you will achieve them. In other words, what are your main goals, and how do you plan to achieve them? What will you need to do? To help you, I will present lots of ideas and suggestions in the following pages that will make this process very easy for you. You can select ideas from my suggested list of things to do or use my list as a springboard for your own unique ideas.

The next step in this process is to set a reasonable timeframe to achieve your goals. For instance you may decide to get out and socialize more. That's a great idea, so when are you going to start?

You may decide to join a choir and/or learn how to play a musical instrument, so when are you going to start? You may decide to do a course, so, when are you going to start looking, and when do you want to complete the course?

It is important to plan ahead, but we should begin the process immediately. This will be easy when we break our plan, goals and objectives down into short, medium and long-term plans. We all need to have things to look forward to, but these things will never happen unless we plan for them. Having long range goals help to take our minds off of our present short-term sadness. It is very important to always have goals and dreams to look forward to.

Isn't it exciting to think about, and wait in wonder, for what may be waiting for you, just around the corner?

Decide to make the best of and enjoy each and every day of your life! Make each new day even better than the day before, and the days you have left behind. Our lives are made up of what we think and do today, not our intentions. Your future joy is down to what you decide to seek and plan for, but more importantly, it is down to what you decide to take action on!

"Actions speak louder than thoughts or words"

Unhealthy Responses to Loss

Before we proceed to take positive actions in overcoming our losses, we need to pause and be honest with ourselves by facing up to whether we have been using unhealthy coping methods up until now?

These include all types of things such as, drinking too much, smoking, taking drugs, forming other addictive habits, promiscuity, unhealthy relationships, surfing sex sites on the internet, having deviant tendencies and/or carrying them out, shutting ourselves off from the world, stopping healthy activities such as exercise, being cynical about everything, working too hard, not having balance in your life, falling into a deep depression, having suicidal tendencies, and many more unhealthy thoughts or activities that do nothing meaningful to help us to move forward to health and wellness.

Some of us may take on these bad unhealthy habits as a means of distraction from our grief and emotional pain. These bad habits may temporarily distract us and numb our sadness for very short periods, but as said before, unresolved grief and its associated sadness and depression will always be lurking in the background waiting to surface and when it does, it will stay with us for much longer periods than the much shorter periods of distraction and numbness.

"The voyage of self-discovery is not seeking new fixes, but in having new eyes"

You may relate to some of the above unhealthy habits or you may know or suspect that someone else may have fallen into one or more of them. If that is the case, you need to deal sensitively and in a caring loving way with the situation, whether it is with yourself or someone else.

None of us like to be reminded of, or to have it pointed out to us, that we have a bad habit, therefore dealing with this situation takes great care and compassion and can only be approached from a place of love, rather than criticism.

One way of doing this for ourselves and suggesting to others is what I call 'The Parent Child Conversation'.

Find a quiet and private place where you can have a chat with yourself where you play both parts, parent and child. Use a note pad to write down important keywords that are used during the conversation. You can then refer back to these in case you forget them, and they will form a record of the main points of your conversations.

Ensure there are no distractions, such as a television in the background. Don't answer the telephone and don't have your mobile phone in the room. This will be a serious conversation that will require your full and honest attention. It deserves to be done without any distractions whatsoever. The outcome of this conversation can be life transforming!

Plan and prepare for this conversation in advance. Write down how you are going to approach the issue and the questions you, as a caring loving parent; intend to ask your child. This exercise is so important that you will need to make time to perform this task. It is more important than any other social engagement you could be doing.

When you have decided how to approach and bring up the subject with your child and when you have listed the questions you intend to ask your child, you are ready to begin.

It would be helpful to set the scene by sitting on a couch and imagine that your child is sitting beside you. Begin the conversation with your child.

You could start by saying "Thank you for taking the time to be with me this evening, I asked to sit down with you because I care for you and love you dearly. I recognize that you are going through a bad period at the moment, and I would like to help you get through it. I have noticed some changes in your behavior and was wondering if you were aware of them, this is not a criticism, I was just wondering"? Pause and wait for the question to sink in. Move to the other side of the couch and play the role of your child.

Child responds, "What do you mean"?

Parent, "Well I can't help noticing that you have been spending a lot of time in your room lately, in fact, as soon as you come home, you go into your room and stay there all night, are you aware of that"?

Child, "I suppose you are right, but there is a lot on my mind at the moment".

Parent, "Let's use this quiet time to talk about what's on your mind, we can work through this together and find ways that will help, what's bothering you the most"?

This is an example of how to start the process. This exercise can be applied to a friend talking to a friend and can include any of the bad behaviors referred to above. It could be a parent talking with a teenager. It could be a family member talking to another family member. It could be a counselor talking to a client. You can apply this exercise in any given situation.

Try it, it may work for you, where you are playing both parts yourself, as part of your own self-help therapy, or you can apply it in a real situation with someone you would like to help. It may be that additional help will be required from a counselor or a therapist, but it is worth a try, as the first step on yourself or on someone else who may seek help from you.

"The greatest gift we can give ourselves or anyone is the energy we invest".

"It's not what we get that's important, it's what we give".

Overindulgence of any kind, bad habits and addictions are usually a reaction to past and/or present situations that have not been dealt with in a healthy manner. Unresolved issues prevent growth and our capacity to move on. Don't be a prisoner to your present or past fears. Fear is lovelessness, of ourselves, of others or our situation. Fear can lead to obsessiveness and addictions. We all need to be aware of this. We all need to reflect on the disadvantages of unhealthy coping mechanisms and the effect they have on our health, wealth, and clarity of mind, our alertness, our energy and the overall impact on our minds, body and souls.

Insanity of inappropriate actions, is to continue doing the same things and expecting to get different results. Give yourself permission to begin anew, and encourage others to do the same. The purpose of life is to grow into our perfection. Think ahead, believe in yourself, and never give up!

You can do it!
By
Alin Austin

Look within and listen to your heart.

You can do it. You can reach that goal.

You can make a new reality instead of accepting things the way they used to be.

You can do it.

All of your highest hopes are with you. Nothing will hold you back but your own fears.

And if you created those fears, they can be dealt with by you and said goodbye to.

You can do it.

Say it to yourself and believe it in your heart.

Make every single day a positive new start, leading to a better and brighter tomorrow.

You can do it. You really can!

###

"All that matters most in life and from our past, is the genuine love we gave and received, everything else pales to insignificance in comparison".

"All of our past is gone, but we can hold on to and treasure its beauty and the blessings we received".

"A blessing from our past is that it got us here, where we have the opportunity to begin all over again".

I recommend that you start each day with morning prayers/ affirmations, and that you include the following in your prayers/ affirmations to God.

"Dear Lord, I give myself permission to begin again".

"Today, I anticipate and welcome new experiences, new blessings and a new life".

Moral Inventory

In addition to my recommendation to begin each day with positive affirmations or what some people refer to as prayer, I also recommend reviewing each day at some point in the evening or before retiring to sleep. Doing a review at the end of your day helps to monitor your progress in how well you are doing and helps to remind you of your blessings and accomplishments.

Later on in this book I will also suggest lists that you can create to help you in moving forward in all kinds of positive ways. This can be part of an exciting journey in more ways than one. By following my recommendations and suggestions you can become a remarkable person, better than you have ever been before. So, let's begin this exciting journey in self-awareness and discovery, which will lead to much peace and joy.

For people who are serious about growing up emotionally and growing spiritually, they need to change bad habits, in-appropriate patterns and negative thinking, and replace these negative traits with positive thoughts and actions. They need to eliminate the negative and develop the positive.

People who want to move on from grief, loss and perhaps dishonesty, deceit, depression, fear, doubt and negativity, would be taking steps in the right direction, if they started to think about their own moral integrity and understand what it means.

Moral integrity has to do with having decent values and principles by which to live your life. These values and principles will help you to grow up emotionally and spiritually. They will help you make decisions about what is right and wrong. They will help you to know what is important in life and what really matters.

Moral integrity will help you find happiness, contentment and perhaps even real love.

"Happiness is a how, not a what, a talent, not an object".

"How we achieve is as important as what we want to achieve".

"Success can be obtained by the person we become".

Success is not so much what we have, it is more about who we are, what we are, but more importantly, it is what we do. Happiness and contentment is not an accident, nor is it something you wish for. Happiness and contentment is something you create!

"You cannot speak that which you do not know. You cannot share what you do not feel. And you cannot give what you do not possess. To give it and share it, and for it to be effective and true, you first need to have it!"

Bad habits, liabilities, negative traits and the dark side of our mind is like an overgrown garden, if we are not careful, the bugs and the weeds of negativity will move into the garden and take away everything of value. You yourself, your family and your love must be cultivated like a garden. Time, effort and attention must be constantly applied to keep it flourishing and growing healthy.

Disgust and resolve are two of the great emotions that lead to change.

Learning is the beginning of health. Learning is the beginning of spirituality. Searching and Learning is where miracles begin. A daily moral inventory is a good place to start. In your own life, thoughts and actions, constantly look for:

Liabilities :	versus	Assets
Resentment		**Forgiveness**
Self-Pity		**Self-Forgetfulness**
Self-Importance		**Modesty**
Self-Justification		**Humility**
Self-Condemnation		**Self Valuation**
Dishonesty		**Honesty**
Impatience		**Patience**
Hate		**Love**
Laziness		**Activity**
Procrastination		**Promptness**
Insincerity		**Straightforwardness**
Negative thinking		**Positive thinking**
Immoral trashy thinking		**Spiritual clean thinking**
Criticising		**Look for the good!**
Lacking generosity		**be more generous**
Being ungrateful		**be more grateful**

The above Liability/Asset List was developed by Alcoholics Anonymous. It is used by leading recovery groups and individuals all over the world with great success. I invite you to review this list and see if there are some areas that you can improve on, and perhaps you can think of other liabilities that are holding you back from becoming a better person in areas of moral integrity?

A great deal of unhappiness and sadness in life can be caused by our lack of moral integrity, our lack of values and our lack of principles.

We all need to let go of bad habits and liabilities and invite a new life of assets into our present and future. By letting go of the negatives of the past, we make room for more blessings and miracles. To do this we must relinquish thoughts of judgement and criticism about anyone or anything that still holds us in the past. This is particularly important regarding our future relationships.

"Accentuate the positive and eliminate the negative".

"Eliminate the bad and develop the good".

"Practice the good and be good!"

Honesty and Truth

Having addressed the subject of morality, it is impossible to proceed further without covering the subjects of integrity and truth, because they are intertwined with each other.

Integrity and truth are inextricably linked. Integrity has to do with honesty, and truth obviously has to do with honesty.

Integrity is also about adherence to moral and ethical principles. It's about soundness of moral character, honesty, truthfulness and uprightness. It's about a sound, unimpaired, perfect condition that we should all aspire to. It's about probity, honor and virtue.

Integrity is the opposite of dishonesty, falsehood, deceit and corruptness.

If we are serious about improving our lives in every respect, and if we are serious about doing a personal moral inventory, we cannot overlook addressing how we rate on the integrity and honesty scale. By doing this we will learn far more about our character, strengths and weaknesses that will go beyond our desire to get over any kind of loss. Many of us overlook these important facts when it comes to personal and spiritual development, as we strive to move forward to growth and new beginnings. Facing up to our deficiencies can be painful. But this is a necessary step. You will learn a lot about yourself by doing a moral inventory and examining how you rate on the integrity and honesty scale. And remember, you can change any aspect of your character, by deciding to change those aspects now. You will not change overnight and the journey may take time, but it will be worth it!

What is truth?

Truth has to do with what is real. It is not about what we perceive, imagine or what we would like it to be.

Real has to do with the existence of the conformity of something. In other words, the actual existence of something in form rather than an idea in someone's mind. Real can be confirmed by more than one source. Real has certainty and can usually be supported by proof. It goes beyond probability and imagination.

There are things that exist that go beyond ones capacity to experience or sense them. For example, if you have never ventured outside of your home, does this mean that the rest of the world doesn't exist? Light exists despite a blind person not seeing light. Real has qualities and substance. Others can verify it. Real can be verified by science.

What is real is not a perception or the basis for a philosophical argument. Real is not just an idea. A debate about the idea of 'real' cannot withstand the scrutiny of 'actuality'. In other words, what has actually happened, the mass of knowledge, the consistency, quality, independent confirmation, evidence, and so on, that can confirm the actual existence of something.

I remember meeting someone who argued that the holocaust didn't actually take place; he argued that it was just an idea, a perception of what actually took place. I rest my case. Real can be verified.

Real has a natural feel. If we are of sound mind, we sense this intuitively. 1+1=2, not 3. We just know and accept this truth. Real makes sense, it has certainty, and it is credible. Truth has objective external corroboration, rather than one's internal mental perceptions.

"Reality is beyond perception".

"How we perceive it, does not make it real".

How to tell when someone is dishonest?

Truth has consistency, dishonesty is full of inconsistencies. Truth can usually be verified. Dishonesty lies in ambiguity and evasiveness. People who seek the truth want to examine details, whilst dishonest people want to skirt over the issues quickly and not dwell on them in case they get caught out. Truth has an essence to it, a quality that feels right, whereas lies leave many unanswered questions. Truth has finality about it, whereas dishonesty remains open to suspicion. When truth is being told, the speaker's flow of thoughts and words are fluent and continuous, whereas, a liar will usually deviate and go off the subject matter and answer unasked questions.

Truth usually has a ring of honesty about it. Truth usually sits easy in your gut. Your intuition, your gut feeling can play an important part in recognizing the truth. Truth has credibility. People seeking the truth don't mind dwelling on it to establish it, while on the other hand, liars want to skip over the issue and circumvent the truth at every opportunity. Truth makes sense; it has universality about it. Truth is what's real!

Truth stands the test of time.
Truth is always simple and uncomplicated.
Truth has beauty.
Truth is beyond doubt.
Truth is sincere.
Truth is genuine.
Truth is pure.

For the pure in heart, the quest of humankind has always been to discover the truth.

> *"An admirable pursuit of mankind is to always pursue justice, peace and truth".*

Facing truths about ourselves and others can be a tremendous help, not only in getting over our losses, but in helping to discover ourselves, who we really are and what aspects we may need to change, as well as identifying traits in others that don't match what we value or seek with respect to morals, values and integrity.

"One secret to success is to spend time with people who share the same pure values, principles and morals that you do".

Grieving over Relationships

This is the hardest grief of all to get over because of its impact and implications on us. There is grief caused by death and then there is the grief of a lost relationship that felt dear to us. In either situation we will all go through some or all of the stages described earlier. This chapter will focus on relationships in general, the good and not so good aspects of relationships and is intended to give you insight that will assist you now and into the future.

Healthy, loving, caring and genuine relationships are the most important thing in life, along with our own health and well-being. They give us the most joy and happiness that cannot be compared to anything else. These relationships include: marriage, partnerships, family, friends, acquaintances and good employers. When any of these relationships end, it is normal and healthy to feel a sense of loss and its associated grief.

If we have contributed to any of these losses, it is important to reflect and learn from them, in order not to make the same mistakes in the future. Please remember the **3 Steps** referred to in a previous chapter, they are: **acknowledge the loss, accept the loss, and take action** about the loss. These steps will be the focus of this chapter on relationships.

It may be that you were not the major contributor to the breakup of a relationship; ironically, this can make it harder to deal with, as you may already possess many of the attributes that contribute to a lasting loving caring relationship. It may be that your partner was not ready, willing or able to contribute their fair share of energy and commitment into your relationship. It may be that despite your efforts, things didn't work out and you feel a sense of rejection. Rejection can cause a deep sense of loss. A person can feel rejection as an attack on their feelings of self-worth and confidence. It is normal to feel this way for a short while, yet we must (having done everything we possibly can) accept the loss and move on, when we come to realize that the other person was just not at the same place we were in and they were not ready, willing or able to make it work, at that time in their life.

Sometimes after a breakup in a relationship, when the initial trauma has subsided and we have had a chance to reflect honestly on the past relationship, we may come to realize that in truth, it may not have been a good relationship after all, and that rather than it seeming to be a setback at the time, it was actually a blessing in disguise to help us move forward and into other meaningful and more genuine relationships. Loss of any kind, including relationships can often be an opportunity for inspiration and creativity.

"Don't cry because it's over, smile because it was".

*"Don't dwell on who let you down,
cherish those who hold you up".*

*"Find someone with similar values, morals
and principles as yourself".*

Aspects of healthy relationships

The fundamental key to a long lasting healthy relationship is to have similar **values**, **morals** and **principles** as your partner. Everything else is secondary to this important fact; yet, this is the most overlooked fact and the main reason for failed relationships and divorce. This is why I addressed these aspects in the preceding chapter.

When we first meet a prospective partner, and start dating, we rarely discuss morals, values and principles. Usually we are initially attracted to looks, sex and other attractions. We rarely explore morals, values and principles. Yet these key fundamental issues are what will eventually make or break the relationship.

We may meet someone in a noisy nightclub, under the influence of drink and/or drugs. Have a dance, feel an attraction and/or just lust, get a phone number or strike it lucky on the night, take the other person home or make a future date with them, sleep with them on the night or as soon as we can, and then continue in a similar pattern without ever having a serious chat about our compatibility regarding our shared or unshared values, morals and principles.

We may continue the interludes, by meeting for dates, dinner, or night clubbing. We may go away for week-ends, social gatherings, and functions, enjoy ourselves, but we may never have serious getting to really know each other discussions. Then we think that all this fun is great and would like it to be permanent, so we decide to enter a long-term relationship or even get married.

Then once we are in a long-term relationship or marriage and spend more time with each other, which will involve learning a lot more about each other, we discover that we are incompatible with fundamental aspects of values, morals and principles. Apart from the fun we had when we were dating, we discover that our belief systems and values are completely at odds with each other, and we wonder why our relationship breaks up.

We may find that our upbringing was vastly different, that our faith/religious values are completely different, and that the things we are passionate about and that feel really important to us are different, and so on. And we wonder what went wrong, why the relationship didn't last? Well you probably know the answer by now, it's because you didn't establish from the very start if you shared the same values, morals and principles. This is important to do!

Don't get me wrong. It's good that you had fun; you may have had a good sex relationship. You may have enjoyed many things together, but many of these things will not last forever, whereas, when we don't have sex as frequently as we would like, when we don't go out clubbing anymore, when having fun and good times are curtailed by raising a family or other responsibilities, when the honeymoon is over, when we lose our health, and so on, all we have left is companionship with someone who may not share the same values, morals and principles. When this happens we feel somewhat alone to say the least. I cannot overstress how important it is in relationships that people share similar values, morals and principles.

I know there are other reasons for breakups, such as violence and abuse in a relationship, money problems and so on, but believe me when I tell you that if your values are in sync with your partner's and when the love and commitment is genuine, you will usually pull through the difficulties that life throws up at you.

You cannot really live in pure harmony with someone who has values diametrically opposed to yours. To ensure success in any relationship, the values, morals and principles of a prospective partner need to be in sync with your own, otherwise it won't work out in the long term. This is a fact!

So what are the ingredients to a long lasting and meaningful relationship?

- **Shared values and interests** A committed relationship needs shared values that anchor and strengthen a relationship.

- **Commitment** Being happy to make a long-term commitment to each other for better or for worse. Commitment in a relationship means commitment to the process of mutual understanding and forgiveness. It means not walking away that lightly.

- **Communication** Communicating with love, honesty, care, sensitivity and compassion. Learning to communicate in a style that works for your partner.

- **Acceptance** Accepting that no one is perfect. That there will be differences, misunderstandings and difficulties. Admitting that we may need to improve in individual ways and together. Admitting that we both need to grow individually, as well as together. Accepting as a team what life throws at us. Accepting challenges by facing them together.

- **Practicality** Being practical as well as being idealistic.

- **Respect** Respect for each other, and the commitments we make to each other.

- **Loyalty** To your partner as well as yourself.

- **Caring** Even when it hurts.

- **Faithfulness** Being faithful to your relationship and your commitments.

- **Support** Supporting each other in every possible way

- **Naturalness** A feeling that it all seems right, natural and appropriate.

- **Harmony** A feeling that most aspects of the relationship are in harmony and feel right.

- **Wholeness** A feeling that the totality of the relationship makes sense and that the wholeness of the relationship is better than being alone.

- **Longing** Having a healthy longing for your partner. Missing them when they are not around. Wanting to be with them as much as possible without smothering them. Healthy longing is not the same as obsession or co-dependence.

- **Letting go of the past** Being prepared to move forward with your partner without carrying baggage from the past. Letting go of mistakes and grudges and a longing to move forward together for better or worse. Not bringing up issues from the past. It may mean letting go of the 'old form' of the relationship and developing a 'new form'.

- **Genuineness** Being genuine in your motives. Trusting each other and communicating honestly. Not playing a game. Being serious about your relationship and the commitment you have made to each.

- **Non-Domineering** Believing that relationships are equal partnerships.

- **Non-Obsessiveness** Being balanced and not being co-dependent or obsessive.

- **Trust** You can't have a relationship with someone you don't trust.

- **Faith** Having optimistic faith in right and wholesome outcomes in your relationship.

- **Hope** Expecting what you truly want is compatible and will turn out for the best.

- **Charity** Giving without counting or expecting anything in return. In addition to helping each other in every possible way, being kind, considerate, caring and compassionate to each other, it all comes back to genuine love, **Unconditional Love** for each other.

The ultimate objective and fulfillment in an intimate close relationship is that we find the meaning of, and practice pure love.

> *"And in the end, the love you take is*
> *equal to the love you make"*
> The Beatles

The above is a summary of what are the essential ingredients to a successful relationship. This may help you to ponder on how well you have contributed to previous relationships, but more importantly, it will help you to be reminded of or become aware of what will be important in future relationships to help them succeed.

Perceived Loss in a Relationship

Sometimes what we perceive as a loss is actually a gain. This section is for people who are grieving over what they thought was a loss, when in fact it may have been the best thing that ever happened to them.

No relationship is or ever will be perfect, because perfection is subjective, an idea in our minds. No one is or will ever be capable of living up completely to someone else's perception of perfection. Relationships are about good and bad, love and hate, joy and sadness, elation and disappointment, give and take. What is important for a successful relationship of any kind, whether it be personal, social or work, is that the assets of the relationship are greater than the liabilities. And when you look honestly at the relationship, if things are not working out now, you have to be confident that there is reasonable probability that things can improve in the future. If you have genuinely tried everything to improve the relationship, it may be better to let it go.

We may stay in an unhealthy relationship out of fear of an unknown future. We may be afraid of being lonely. We may lack confidence to face changes. We may have become co-dependent on our partner. But if we decide and plan for what we want in the future there is no need for fear, instead, we should become excited about our future possibilities and prospects. If we become busy by doing some of the things recommended in this book, we won't have the time to be lonely because we will be too busy having fun. If we use this book like a road map by applying the tips, hints, suggestions and recommendations, we will have all of the confidence we need to break free from unhealthy relationships and never feel co-dependent on anyone ever again.

The Quantum Collapse Process

Dr. John Demartini is credited with developing this process which he has published a book about and which he gives seminars and workshops on. I found it to be a very enlightening process that helps us to look at issues of relationships, perceptions, letting go, and moving on. The process helps us to have a balanced view of these issues and I share the basic concepts with you for whatever help they may give you.

Demartini suggests asking ourselves serious challenging questions that cause us to reflect on important issues in our lives and that our honest answers will enable us to have a better perspective on life in general. He maintains that many of us have lopsided perceptions that we allow or have allowed to run our lives, our wealth, our relationships, our self-worth and self-confidence. He argues that these out of balance perceptions are often the main reason why things have not turned out, as we would have preferred. He maintains that answering the following questions will help us rebalance our lives and have a better perspective on things in general.

He suggests that power is energy and that as a result of lopsided perceptions we deny ourselves our own energy, waste it and give it away to other situations and people that don't deserve it. Valuable energy that could be applied to more deserving things and more deserving people. What you put your energy into grows, the reverse is also true. The greatest gift you can give to others is your positive energy. Relationships won't work unless both parties put positive energy into the relationship. Therefore, if your investment of time and energy into something or anyone isn't working, it's time to apply it to people and things that will give you a better return on your investment.

Why give ex-partners, former employers, etc., any more time and energy than we have already given them? Our energy can be compared to our SPIRIT, which is a very precious gift that we should not waste on undeserving people or issues.

If we have already given our energy, our undivided love, our attention, our everything to another person, job, or whatever, we should have no reason to feel any guilt that things didn't work out. If we have been hurt by others, we need to discover why we feel that way, acknowledge it, learn from it and move on, leaving the resentment, sadness, bitterness and anger behind us.

You have to have faith, confidence, and trust in someone, to have a close relationship with that person that has the potential to last. If that has not been the case in the past and if it is unlikely to happen in the future (assuming you are doing all the right things to help make it happen), then you need to accept this reality and move on and make it happen with someone else. This scenario also applies to friendships and relationships of any kind, including employer and professional relationships and associations.

"What seems a loss is often a gain"

> *"When things don't work out, it's time*
> *to do things differently".*

Endings and Beginnings

Charles Dickens suggested that life is a series of partings. I maintain that for every parting there is an opportunity for more meetings. I believe that more meetings will help you eventually find your true destiny! I believe that for every ending, there are always opportunities for new beginnings. Many endings often turn out to be milestones in our journey through life and turn out to be the best for all concerned. These endings often lead to new beginnings that become better than you could have ever imagined. It is a matter of having faith, hope and confidence.

When a loved one dies, after a period of respectful mourning, we need to release their spirit to heaven, honor and respect them for the love, light, laughter and happiness that they brought into our life and begin to look for the positive traits they possessed in others. You will recognize them when you are open to looking for and seeing them in others.

> *"Let today and every day be a vision of hope".*

> *"There is a difference between hope and wishful thinking".*

> *"Often in life you have no choice but to be patient, because*
> *there is often a greater destiny for you. Think of the*
> *exhilaration and excitement of waiting patiently to see*
> *what just might be around the corner, waiting for you".*

Wisdom and psychology show us that what we feel, we see all around us. In other words, if we feel fear, we will see it everywhere. If we feel love, we will see it everywhere. The same goes for good and bad. What we see out there in the world, and all around us, is often a reflection of how we feel inside. What we admire and detest in others is usually what we love and hate about ourselves. When we are attracted to others (apart from admiring their physical beauty), it is usually their traits, their manner, and their positive energy that we are attracted to. Needless to say, what turns us off people is their negative behaviors and their negative energy, the areas we dislike about ourselves.

Carl Jung, the brilliant 20th. Century psychiatrist says, that until we can come to terms with all of our qualities, the good and the bad, the divine and the diabolical, we can never become whole. At times we have all been both saint and sinner, this does not mean that we have to accept and hold on to being a sinner forever, it just means that we have to acknowledge this in ourselves and others, forgive ourselves and others for the times we have been diabolical in the past, learn from our mistakes and take personal responsibility for letting go of the bad aspects of our lives and move forward towards being better. Life is a process of continuous growth.

Demartini suggests that we are here to master seven areas in our lives:
- Spiritual
- Mental
- Vocational
- Financial
- Social
- Physical
- Family

I maintain that we need to add the following:
- Values
- Principles
- Morals
- Integrity
- Health
- Love

We will look at these core elements individually and I will explain what they mean. When we master all of these core areas, our lives will be transformed beyond our greatest dreams. We will be happier and live more fulfilled lives. We will attract what we want, in love, relationships, wealth, health and contentment. You will become more confident.

Spirituality is an essential dimension that each of us needs to explore and develop. The greatest people who ever lived all eventually came to realize the importance and help that this dimension gave them when they realized that they needed to connect with an energy that was greater than themselves alone. God created everything. You are a unique gift from God. You are a part of God and God's creation. When you seek to understand and realize this, it will help you. Spirituality is universal rather than a particular religious dogma.

Mental ability is something we need to constantly develop, which means improving our intelligence and constantly learning about others, ourselves, and what works and what doesn't.

Vocation has to do with our inclinations towards work, a job, a career and/or a profession. We need to find a job or a role in life that will provide us with security and a sense of achievement and if this means we need more education, we need to get it. We may need to update our skills or acquire new skills by doing training courses, seminars, or higher education. It may be beneficial to get help from a counselor or career guidance consultant.

Financial means that we need to focus on economic stability for ourselves and/or our dependents. We need to acquire wealth legitimately such as earning money honestly.

Social means that we need to be more social, make friends, develop networks and support groups. It means getting out there and getting involved with others.

Physical means that we need to look our best at all times. We need to be as physically healthy as we can be, which may mean going on a diet and dressing better. This will make us feel better and will make us more attractive to others.

Family means that we need to pay more attention to our family. We need to become more aware of their needs and do everything in our power to meet their needs. We need to resolve differences and work towards improving our relationship with our family. Blood is thicker than water and at the end of the day, when all your friends may not be around, it would be nice to have a family to help you in times of need.

Values, principles, morals and integrity have been addressed earlier in this book.

Health means physical as well as emotional.

Love. Last but not least, the most important thing to master in our lives is **LOVE**.

Everything we attempt to master must be done under the heading of love. Love for ourselves, as well as love for all.

When we begin to master these core elements in our lives under the guiding light of love, we will be on the right track. Before you attempt any task in life ask yourself the question "Am I doing this because I love myself enough, or am I doing this because I love another person or others enough"? If they answer is yes, your motives are pure.

Fear. It is said that love is the opposite of fear. Fear is an illusion that can prevent us from moving forward. Fear can keep us living in the past. Fear is an assumption that you may experience more pain than pleasure, more negative than positive, more loss than gain.

Fear is an overwhelming perception of loss and pain. If you created the fear or allowed it to exist, you can release it and turn the pain into gain and fear into love.

It is ironic that the main causes of fear in our lives is the lack of love and the absence of some of the core elements described above. The good news is that as soon as we begin to master the above core elements, we will begin to remove most of the fears in our life and they will be replaced by love. You can do it, you really can!

Here are the types of questions that Demartini suggests we ask about our relationships and ourselves:

- What are the three top griefs in your life right now?
- What are you doing about them?

- Who is controlling your life right now?
- Who or what pushes your buttons the most right now?
- **Who** do you see as being in your way right now?
- **What** do you see as being in your way right now?
- Who hurt you?
- Who do you feel incomplete with?
- Who are you having difficulty loving right now and why?
- What is it about this person that that makes them unlikable right now?
- What is it that this person has done or not done that makes you feel so bad and why?
- Who do you resent the most right now?
- Who left you, abandoned you or dumped you?
- Who do you despise right now?
- Who are you trying to avoid right now and why?
- When you think about people who hurt you, why do you feel hurt?
- What traits in people do you hate the most?
- What are the benefits of recognizing traits in others that you dislike?
- What human traits do you feel you lost?
- What has the other person done that you have not?
- Who acted out the human traits you dislike in others?
- Who has now taken on some of the traits you most hate in others?
- Have you mirrored to others what you dislike?

Regarding the person we most admire at the moment:
- What traits do you most like about this person?
- What is it about this person that makes them likable?
- What has this person done that made you feel so good?
- What is it about this person that you admire?

Regarding the people we like:
- Why are you attracted to people with good traits?

- Why do you want to connect with people with good traits?
- Why is it important to associate with people who have good traits?
- Why is it essential to find a partner with good traits?
- Do you want to start looking for good traits in others?
- Are you ready to look for good characteristic traits in others?
- Are you ready to develop good characteristic traits, morals and values in yourself?

In the book 'The Secret' it covers the important elements of 'the law of attraction', 'matching values' and the purity of 'intentions'. When these elements are in sync in relationships, they determine whether things feel good or bad and they help us to decide whether we should leave or stay in a relationship.

At this stage, you should now be in a better state of mind to decide whether you're perceived important failed relationship can be re-built? Is worth re-building or whether it is best to move on to start a new one? Either way, you will become a better person by applying what you learn in this book, and you will be well on your way to finding your true and ultimate destiny.

"When one door closes, others open".

"Time and circumstance determines who comes into your life. Your mind, body and spirit determine whom you would like to stay in your life. Your actions determine who remains in your life".

"Never lose yourself, while trying to hold on to someone who doesn't care about losing you"
Mhar

"If you don't miss me, others do. If you don't love me, others will".

"Life is too short to waste a single second on anyone who doesn't appreciate or value us".

"Find and hold on to the one who picks you up when you fall down".

"People who are meant to be with each other will be".

"Sometimes things don't happen to us, they happen for us".

Positive Mental Attitudes

It's difficult to get over any loss and move forward if our past experiences are still causing us to feel negative, worried, upset and bitter. Negative thoughts take away our energy, and they greatly affect our attitude.

"In life, we are passengers of our own attitudes, whether they are negative or positive".

"Attitudes make you who you are".

Attitudes determine what you think and you are defined by what you think. Negative thoughts give off negative energies. The energy you give off, will either turn people on or off you.

"Positive thinking creates positive energy which attracts positive energy to you"

You can't wake up each day and decide how you are going to feel based on whether something will happen or not that will cause you to feel happy and positive. If something nice happens to you, by all means feel happy and be grateful, but you should still develop a positive frame of mind to help you manage and cope with the unhappy times that you will have to deal with.

Don't be a victim to negative thinking and emotions that can control you, run and ruin your life. Take control of your own life by adapting a positive healthy mental attitude that will naturally attract positive things into your life.

You can decide, by your attitude, to make Monday mornings feel as good as Friday afternoons. It's all a matter of attitude. Positive minds are attracted to each other; therefore, surround yourself by positive people who can inspire you, rather than spending time with negative people who can pull you down.

"If you look for beauty, you will find it in people, things and places".

Everything revolves around energy, whether positive or negative. We sense this when we meet and speak to people. It's often referred to as a vibe. It's something we feel. It's something our intuition picks up on. We all should ask ourselves the following question "What vibes am I giving off"? This is especially important if we don't seem to make friends easily.

So, the answer to overcoming our own negative energy is to develop a positive mental attitude. This means letting go of negativity and upset. Focus on what you want rather than on what you don't want. Focus on who you would like to be rather than who you were.

Think happy, feel happy and be happy! Act happy and smile! Feel good, be good and attract good! Think of your positive attributes. Think of your blessings. Think of what you can do to contribute to life and life situations. Think of how you can help others. Think of how lucky you are and what you have to offer.

Taking Positive Actions

"Make realistic achievable goals. Plan to achieve them. Set realistic timeframes. Achieve them!"

"Whatever goals you set for yourself, the beginning, the first step, starts with you!"

"Your first step starts in your mind"

Your thoughts can become achievements. Think about what you really want and if it is realistic, focus your thoughts and energies on your goal and it will usually be achieved. This principle also applies to multiple goals. Positive thinking creates positive energy in yourself, which in turn, will attract positive energy to you. Focus on what you want, not what you don't want.

When you come up against obstacles and challenges in achieving your goals, eliminate your personal feelings, emotions and frustrations, stay focused on the goals that you want to achieve and your positive thinking and energy will help you overcome the temporary hurdles.

Believe in your own abilities, capabilities and potential. Sometimes you will temporarily fail or trip up, but the same positive strategy will enable you to try again and keep on trying until you do succeed.

*"Never give up when you have more to give. It's
only over when you don't give anymore".*

*"There are times in life when we can't be bothered,
when we give up trying, and loose our way, but
we still must do what we know is right".*

*"No one can make things perfect, but
we can all make things right".*

Share your goals with others who may be able to help you.
Build support networks that will assist you in reaching your goals.
Have a healthy balance to your goals. Break big goals into little
ones that can easily be achieved one step at a time. Keep your
goals practical.

Set your goals, and plan your course of actions. Be specific;
put your goals down on paper. Track and monitor your progress
towards attaining your goals.

*"Remember, our lives are made up of what we
think, say and do, not just our intentions".*

"Just thinking about it, doesn't boil the rice".
Old Chinese Proverb

"Conceive, believe, achieve".
Napoleon Hill

How to Mend a Wounded Heart

Following a loss or any kind can cause us to feel wounded. Whether it is the loss of a relationship, a friendship, job, a home, our wealth, our health, whatever the loss may be. Note that I used the term 'wounded' rather than 'broken'. You may have heard the phrase "his/her heart was broken" in reference to a failed relationship. I use the term "wounded' because what is wounded can almost always be fixed, on the other hand, sometimes what has been broken can't be fixed.

The advice in this chapter, and in this book overall, can be used for the reader to help themselves, and it can be used by a reader to help others. It is universal guidance to help everyone get over loss of almost any kind and to help them mend their own wounded hearts, or to help others mend their wounded hearts.

A wounded heart can cause the same feelings and emotions as loss, some of these include, profound sadness, sorrow, stress, anxiety and depression. The following advice will help to heal a wounded heart.

Assess the situation that is causing you to feel wounded. Look beyond your emotions and feelings to the facts connected with the situation. For example, "I know you are feeling sad and gloomy right now, that's obvious to everybody, but what aspect of your sorrow is making you feel so low"? In other words, find specifics for the wounded heart. Often the real issues are below the surface, so you need to find the underlying issues, the heart of the matter. Let me give you an example.

Mary is very sad and sorrowful. She split up with her boyfriend who suffered depression and as a result of his deep depression, which he didn't seek any help for, he just got up one day and walked out of her life. Mary and her boyfriend had recently purchased an apartment together, which they both lived in and shared expenses for. Now Mary is faced with selling the apartment that she cannot afford on her salary alone, and because there is no equity profit in the apartment, she will have to sell it for less than it cost. Mary will also lose $50,000.00 that she put into buying the apartment. Overall, Mary will lose $100,000.00 after she sells the apartment at a loss.

Mary will obviously be sad and stressed about her situation, which she didn't bring about. Mary is now penniless and she doesn't know where she is going to live. Mary has challenges. Now that we have established the real underlying reason for Mary feeling wounded, we can work towards overcoming her challenge in non-emotional practical ways. This is what assessing the situation thoroughly means. <u>Look at the underlying facts of the situation rather than the emotions.</u>

Talk about the situation to close family and friends who will keep the details confidential. They will help and support you by giving you practical suggestions that you have not been able to see clearly because of your own hurt and grief.

Seek professional help if that is required. You may need emotional help from a counselor, therapist or a psychologist. Practical help can be found from Debt Counselors, your Bank Manager, Lawyer, and Family Advice Centers.

Sharing your feelings with others will lessen the burden and not only give you emotional support, but point the way forward to finding practical solutions to your challenges.

Read other self-help books on the areas that you are finding challenging at the moment. There are free Telephone Help Lines. Go to your library and look for books that will help you.

Google topics to find information that may be helpful.

Get healthy in body as well as mind. Start exercising. Go for daily walks. Take up an activity that will exercise your mind as well as your body. Start eating a healthy diet. Make sure that your body and your mind are getting all the essential nutrients and vitamins that they need to stay healthy.

Do fun things that will give you pleasure as well as activity. This will help to take your mind off sadness and negative emotions. Do things that will help you to feel happy! It is impossible to be sad when you are happy. You cannot experience these two feelings at the same time.

Join clubs. Do volunteer work. Visit a day-spa and pamper yourself. Book a weekly full-body massage if you can afford to. Make lists of things that you could do. I will provide a list of ideas in the following pages.

Start implementing some of the ideas presented here and in the following pages and then review how you are progressing and how much better you are feeling. Change and adapt what needs to be changed or adapted in your life.

- Have things to look forward to. Plan holidays and weekend breaks

- Meditate daily or learn to meditate. The benefits of meditation are enormous.

- Say daily affirmations and consider taking up praying which can be a powerful aid to healing for both yourself and others.

- Treat each and every day as if it was going to be your last.

- Start a daily log of your accomplishments and review it regularly to lift your spirits.

- Consider fasting once a week. The benefits of fasting are that you are in control. It builds will power, emotional strength, confidence and helps to de-toxify your body.

- Go on a diet if you are overweight.

- Start dressing better if you have let yourself go a little bit.

- Stay positive and keep faith in yourself.

- Remember that wounds take time to heal. Your wounded heart will heal; it's just a matter of time, as long as you take all of the appropriate actions necessary to heal the wound yourself.

"Do fun things that you enjoy and do them more often".

Setting and Achieving
Realistic Goals

This section is about helping you to achieve realistic goals. Achieving goals is a process. It starts with determining what goals you would like to achieve and as long as they are within your powers and resources, list them down, and then develop strategies on how you can best achieve them. Then muster up all the positive energy you can, think about who can help you, and then devote all your positive energies (including help from others) to implement an action plan to achieve your goals. That's it in a nutshell!

It will help you to reflect on goals that you have achieved in the past. List some of them down. Think about how you started the process in the past. It probably started with an idea, something that you wanted to achieve. What are the steps you took in the past? How and why did things fall into place? How did things that you wanted to happen come into your life in the past? Do you recognize the basic steps summarized above? What were the things that worked in the past? What didn't work in the past? What can you learn from your past achievement of goals that you can apply now? I bet that when you were successful in the past that it was as a result of applying the basic steps naturally and consciously.

So let's have a brief overview of the three basic stages in this process:

1. **Identify what you want to achieve**. Ask yourself: do I really want this? Is this really important to me? Will it make me happy and content? Does it make sense? Will my life improve if I achieve this particular goal? Once you are clear on what you really want, make a list, and move to the next step.

2. **Align your positive mental attitude and energies into achieving your goals**. Use all the resources you can to help you. Feel good about what goals you have set. Think of the positive benefits. Think about how you will feel when you achieve your goals. Visualize your goal; imagine having it right now, then ardently seek it. We usually get what we think, feel and act on, eventually. Be patient!

3. **Take inspired actions to enable you to achieve your goals**. This means listening to your soul, your heart, and responding to your desires by taking all the appropriate steps necessary to achieving your desired results. If your goals are pure and if they are aligned with your genuine intent, morality, principles and integrity, all of your positive actions for achieving your goals will feel right and natural. They will make you feel good. You positive energies will rub off on others and they will help bring into your life those goals that are worthy and that you deserve.

"Goals. There's no telling what you can do when they inspire you. There's no telling what you can do when you believe in them. There's no telling what will happen when you act upon them".
Jim Rohn

Do's for Recovery

- Find inspiration
- Put yourself first (in your own healing and welfare)
- Be kind to yourself
- Believe in yourself
- Take care of yourself as your first priority
- Look after yourself
- Stay clear of negativity
- Reach out and help others, after you have sorted yourself out first
- Help others who feel alone
- Be a mentor to others
- Find mentors for yourself
- Each day do at least three nice things for others as well as yourself
- Compliment yourself and others for something well done
- Brighten other people's days
- Help others who are genuinely worse off
- Help others who have real problems
- Do volunteer work
- Pray daily
- Use daily affirmations
- Do fun things
- Keep active in mind as well as body
- Review your progress

- Walk
- Jog
- Swim
- Get a bicycle and use it
- Socialize more
- Take up hobbies
- Join a choir
- Get fit
- Plan things to look forward to
- Join a church
- Join a support group

- Get out in the sun

More Ideas:

Below is a list of ideas that you could use as appropriate for yourself. Making lists will help you to keep positive and remind you of your blessings.

- List your blessings
- Reflect on your blessings
- -List what makes you feel happy
- What makes you fulfilled?
- Keep a daily and weekly account of your achievements and accomplishments
  If you had your life to live over again what would you do differently?
- List what's wonderful in your life
- What makes you feel alive?
- List your talents
- List what you are good at?
- Do things that work and do them more often
- List what's really important in your life
- What do you have a passion about?
- What would you like to do if you could?
- What do you really need to change in your life?

- What would your wish be if you were only granted one wish?
- What are the priorities in your life?
- Make a list of what you want to achieve in life
- Prioritize
- Make a list of what is of real value to you
- Make a list of your strengths
- Make a list of how you can help others
- Make a list of your qualities
- List strategies, goals and objectives that you believe are crucial for your own happiness and wellbeing.
- List what you have overcome in your life
- Think about what you appreciate in people and above all yourself
- Focus on the good that you want rather than on the bad you don't want
- Live in hope rather than fear
- Think of your abundance
- Think of your strengths
- Think of your talents
- Think of your good qualities
- Think of how you have helped others
- Think of your achievements
- Think of the good deeds that you have done
- Think of how you have helped and whom you have helped in life
- Think of your achievements and accomplishments
- Think about what you can do to help others and society in general
- Think about how you would like to be remembered

When you know what you want, and you want it badly enough, you will usually get it. When you expect miracles, they often happen. Feel as positive and as Good as you can be. Be as positive and as Good as you can be! When you try your best at being positive and good, you will usually attract the same in return.

Focus on your health and being well. Visualize being better and being healthy. It actually helps others by inspiring them to do the same.

Happiness involves joy, excitement, fun, pleasure, contentment, fulfillment, a sense of achievement, being grateful, being confident, being at peace with yourself and others, being optimistic and being determined.

The mnemonic **C.H.A.T**. means being **C**alm, **H**appy, having a positive **A**ttitude and **T**olerance. The mnemonic **C.H.O.O.S.E** means having **C**larity of purpose, **H**ealth, **O**ptimism, **O**thers in your life, developing your **S**trengths and **E**njoying each and every moment. It's now up to you to **CHAT** and **CHOOSE!**

A FEW MORE IDEAS:

- Take up art
- Learn how to play a musical instrument
- Have fun
- Keep yourself occupied
- Seek professional help if necessary
- Do community support work
- Make contact with family and friends
- Go dancing
- Plan a vacation
- Learn a language
- Focus on what you have rather than on what you think you don't have

MAKE A LIST OF YOUR OWN IDEAS BELOW:

Don'ts for Recovery

- Don't attribute blame
- Don't resent
- Don't be bitter
- Don't feel a victim
- Don't criticize
- Don't be judgmental
- Don't seek revenge
- Don't plot
- Don't scheme
- Don't manipulate
- Don't dwell on the negative
- Don' allow yourself to be overwhelmed by negative emotions
- Don't dwell on the past

Summary

Focus on your positive blessings, your talents, your strengths and the things that give you joy. Seek peace for yourself and with others. Do things that give you pleasure, peace and joy. Continue learning and self-development. Explore the spiritual and religious side of your nature. Go to a health farm. Treat yourself to a weekly massage. Go on a retreat. Associate yourself with positive people. Stay positive. Focus on your own well-being. Health permitting, get well! If not, decide to get well anyway. Get well, stay well and be well!

Start a daily log of your accomplishments and constantly review it to lift your spirits. Treat each and every day as if it was going to be your last. Use your intuition and balance it with facts and reality.

Don't wait for happiness to come to you, create it yourself. Relax, smile more often and decide to be as happy as you can. Take things less serious. If you only had a week to live, what would you do? Live your own life on your own terms. Always look on the bright side.

Smile more often. Paddle your own canoe. Get out more often. Go for lots of walks. Get the sun on your face. Fresh air and a good walk can help to lift gloom. Keep your home spotless, bright and fresh. Shutting yourself off from the world is the last thing you need to do when you are feeling sad and depressed. Have a daily routine. Create stability in your life, and remember that there is no such thing as permanent security. Be realistic in all things.

"If you are meant to accomplish something at a particular time, you already have what you need".
"Patience is more than a virtue, it is necessary for a happy life".
"Think ahead, believe in yourself and never give up".

Positive Thoughts for Today and Always

(A daily Morning Affirmation)

I anticipate and welcome new experiences, new life and new blessings today. I am grateful!

Any negative thoughts, depression or discouragement stops here and now.

I anticipate and welcome new experiences of harmony, success and understanding today, I am grateful!

Today, I welcome Joy, Peace, Health, Order, Fulfillment, and to be supplied with what I really need. In return, I will offer the same to others.

Today, I anticipate even greater experiences of Health, Life, New Blessings and Spiritual Understanding. I am grateful!

Today, I will not let circumstances control me. I will stay calm and take control of how I react to situations. I will control my emotions, remain calm and stay in control.

Today, with each new experience, (even if it seems bad), will come a blessing which I can learn from.

God the Creator, loves me right now always does and always will.

I start this day by inviting God's loving grace and care. I open my whole being to the realization that GOD is LOVE, loves me right now; will love me all day long and forever.

I call on God to give me strength and courage to meet every situation this day and to enable me to always give and receive a blessing. I will look for and see blessings everywhere.

Today, I will make myself completely receptive to the love God is pouring out, in, and through me. I will try to pay particular attention to the love I receive from others.

I am glad. As I remember, that throughout this day, that God cares for me and loves me. In return, I will act as a responsible person, and express my care and love to others.

Dear God, please help me to remember, that nothing is going to happen today that you and I cannot handle.

Thank you Lord, for your constant care, love and blessings, for which I am grateful!

Repeat as often as you like, ideally first thing in the morning and throughout the day.

It is a good way to start your day and to keep you positively focused.

"Choose love rather than fear".

Winners Are People like You

By
Nancye Sims

Winners take chances.

Like everyone else, they fear failing, but they refuse to let fear control them.

Winners don't give up.

When life gets rough, they hang on there until the going gets better.

Winners are flexible. They realize there is more than one way and are willing to try others.

Winners know they are not perfect. They acknowledge their weaknesses while making the most of their strengths.

Winners fall, but they don't stay down. They stubbornly refuse to let a fall keep them from climbing.

Winners don't blame fate for their failures, nor luck for their successes.

Winners accept responsibility for their lives.

Winners are positive thinkers who see the good in all things.

From the ordinary, they make the extraordinary.

Winners believe in the path they have chosen even when it's hard, even when others can't see where they are going.

Winners are patient.

They know a goal is only as worthy as the effort that's required to achieve it.

Winners are people like you.

They make the world a better place to be.

"Always have dreams and goals".

"It's what you can do, not what you can't do that's important, the most important".

"Enjoy each and every day of your life and decide to make each new day better than the ones already gone".

"If we don't give up, we will succeed".

"Remember the 3 'F's, Focus, Focus, Focus".

A Reflection on our Life's Journey

In this book, I not only want to help the reader cope with loss, I want to pass on ideas and suggestions that will help you transform your life in general terms as well, assuming you have not already reached perfection.

In my next two books, I will focus on relationship loss and universal laws that will help the reader to transform their lives according to principles and wisdom passed on from Masters, Prophets and Gurus in the areas of personal self-development and enlightenment.

I will share a few of these basic principles with you now.

The essence of our journey here on earth is to discover true love, and that has to begin within us first. We need to love ourselves first before we can truly love another in a healthy way. We need to discover, come to terms with, and address issues that need to be healed within us before we can effectively move forward in our own lives and to be able to help others and personally live a fulfilled life. Taking this step may require more professional help than what is contained in this self-help book. I encourage you to seek this help without hesitation if you can't make the journey on your own.

It is important to establish peace and contentment within ourselves as a primary first goal. We all need to feel comfortable in our own skin and heart. We need to feel as complete as we can within us. We should feel satisfied with how far we have come, to date in our lives. It helps when we discover our gifts and our purpose in life. Life becomes better for us when we strive to be the best we can be and to continually strive to be as good as we can, regarding worthwhile efforts. It is beneficial to realize that part of our journey here on earth is to be of help and to serve others in any reasonable way we can. We all need to realize that we have to develop our own self-confidence rather than expecting it to come from others. We all need encouragement from others, but at the end of the day, we can only develop our own self-confidence and sense of purpose and to establish what is really important in life for us, and our own wellbeing.

> *"When I die, Jesus is not going to ask me what type of job I had, where I lived, how much money I earned a year, which university I went to, or what type of a car I drove, or how many prayers did I say, or even Masses I attended, or anything like that.*
>
> *What he is going to ask is: How did you love those people who traveled life's journey with you?"* Oscar Romero, Homily, 6/11/77, Violence of Love.

###

An Affirmation for your Journey

Dear God, as we journey through this world, give us the grace to allow your Spirit, to work through us.

Help us to speak, think and work with honesty, and compassion, to celebrate all that is life giving, to restore hope where it has been lost, and to bring about change wherever it is needed.

We ask this in your holy name. Amen

In life's journey, always be a friend to yourself as well as others. Support yourself, encourage yourself, and be kind to yourself. Give yourself good counsel. Advise yourself as you would someone you care for.

"If you do your best, whatever happens will be for the best".

"Always remember, that there is no situation in life that doesn't have some good in it!"

"Learn how to be happy with what you have while you pursue all that you need".
Jim Rohn

"There are two ways to face the future. One way is with apprehension; the other is with anticipation".
Jim Rohn

"Occupy yourself with anything other than unhealthy grief or depression".
"With God, all things are possible"
Matthew 19:26

I wish you well in your life journey of overcoming the loss that you have experienced and leave you with an Irish Blessing:

May the road rise to meet you. May the wind always be on your back to help push you along. May the warmth of the Sun smile gently upon your face and may God always hold you in the warmth of his ever presence. May you be and feel richly blessed, always!

Michael Pierce. Melbourne, 2016